# The
# Heart-Wrenching August

Asadullah Jafari "Pezhman"

**Ukiyoto Publishing**

All global publishing rights are held by

**Ukiyoto Publishing**

Published in 2023

Content Copyright © Asadullah Jafari "Pezhman"

ISBN 9789360499693

*All rights reserved.*
*No part of this publication may be reproduced, transmitted, or stored in a retrieval system, in any form by any means, electronic, mechanical, photocopying, recording or otherwise, without the prior permission of the publisher.*

*The moral rights of the author have been asserted.*

*This book is sold subject to the condition that it shall not by way of trade or otherwise, be lent, resold, hired out or otherwise circulated, without the publisher's prior consent, in any form of binding or cover other than that in which it is published.*

www.ukiyoto.com

# Dedication

From all those whom I made them the trouble to write this story, and I have talked and interviewed with them. So, they happily provided me with reliable information about a tragic story so that I could be the voice of a victim who is no longer with us. And I have a special thanks to the esteemed publisher "Ukiyoto Publishing" who accepted the publication and efforts of this work with open arms.

Best regards

Asadullah Jafari "Pezhman"

*Photo Courtesy: QAIS USYAN/AFP*

# Writer's Note

This story is a small part of the realities of terrorism, violence, and war crimes committed by the Taliban against civilians, especially against women and ethnic minorities in Afghanistan. Since I have always been looking for such bitter events in Afghanistan societies and why the sorrows of Afghan women in Afghanistan society are more than their joys, it has always been a vexing but unanswered question. This sad but true story may be painful for the victims of war, but I hope that rereading such stories will also be healing for the victims. I have relatives who live in the western city of Kabul, Afghanistan. They recently shared with me the tragic experience that happened to a Hazara family who lived in their neighborhood. This is a **"True Story"** of violence and torture against a young girl whose brother was a member of the Afghan National Army. This family was under persecution by the Taliban for a long time and finally fell into the deception trap of this group. It may be difficult and sad for some dear readers to read this story, but I hope that I have been able to reflect a small part of human rights violations and crimes against humanity from a corner of this world. Nevertheless, for security reasons and the protection of other family members, some names have been changed in the story and are pseudonyms.

Najiba was one of the thousands of victims of Afghan National Army soldiers' sisters after the brutal Taliban entered the cities of Afghanistan. She was 25 years old and a student of English literature at one of the private universities in Ghazni city on the eve of the fall of Ghazni province in the south-east of Afghanistan to the hands of the Taliban group. Najiba and her family fled to Kabul to save the family, hoping to escape from the war conditions in Ghazni province because her brother was a member of the Afghan National Army.

# Contents

| | |
|---|---|
| Futile Struggles | 1 |
| A Kind Of Hell | 2 |
| Discrimination And Inequality | 3 |
| Gradual Death | 4 |
| Unknown Man | 5 |
| "Najiba Asked Herself" | 9 |
| Rescue Or Entrapment? | 10 |
| Kārte Parwān Place Of Trapping | 11 |
| The Heart-Wrenching August | 13 |
| Brutal And Inhuman Tortures | 15 |
| *About the Author* | *17* |

# Futile Struggles

Najiba and her family took refuge in Kabul city, not knowing that Kabul would soon be handed over to the Taliban terrorist group by corrupt Afghan politicians. Najiba and her brother, who was a member of the Afghan National Army, came to Kabul on August 1, 2021, shortly before the Taliban took power in the Afghanistan capital. And they, like other citizens of Kabul and vulnerable Afghans, tried hard to use the facilities provided by different countries to exit the country. They tried to find a way to save themselves, but all their efforts were fruitless, and there was no hope for them. So, all their efforts to get out of Kabul airport were in vain.

## 2  The Heart-Wrenching August

# A Kind Of Hell

Najiba and her brother tried their luck to leave their motherland, and they had difficulty reaching the Kabul airport, as thousands were trying to get there too. When the Taliban entered Kabul city, the city became a "Kind of Hell" for the citizens of Afghanistan. During the evacuation of vulnerable people from Kabul airport, dozens of people were injured, killed, and missing till today. Even small children were trampled in front of their mothers in the crowd. No one could help anyone; even women and girls were sexually assaulted by unknown and Taliban groups. In the end, Najiba was not spared from this disaster either.

# Discrimination And Inequality

After two days and nights of hunger and thirst, Najiba did not get any results, but her brother, who was an army soldier, was also injured by a Taliban bullet. Both of them returned to the house of one of their relatives in the suburbs of Kabul airport with sadness and longing....

From the time of her birth to her youth, Najiba had always witnessed killing, murder, rape, discrimination, inequality, and despair in this "Ruin" called Afghanistan. She remembered all the atrocities of the Taliban by quoting the stories of her parents. And Now, Najiba herself would be the narrator and protagonist of these events and heartbreaking stories for other generations in the land of Afghanistan.

The collapse of the system in Afghanistan, especially the national army, was the only wish of the sisters of the army soldiers and the people of Afghanistan. And with the Taliban's unexpected control over government offices and institutions, many Afghan girls and women have become victims of this incident and have stayed-at-home.

## 4 The Heart-Wrenching August

# Gradual Death

After two decades, the dark shadow and difficult times under the Taliban's flag have been re-established for all Afghan people, especially women, and girls who want training, education, bread, freedom, work, and equal rights. It is an issue that all dreams of the Afghan people, especially the women, and girls in their lives, have faced a gradual death under the rule of Taliban fundamentalism. It was hard to believe that Afghan civilians and women would once again be under the domination of the religious fundamentalism of the Taliban and would face a gradual death. Therefore, Najiba read on her Facebook suicide news that one of her classmates committed suicide due to frustration and mental pressure. And she noticed many bitter and unfortunate events in Kabul by following them on social media. Among other things, the Taliban had announced that no girl or woman would be allowed to leave their homes without a male mahram (Chaperone). Moreover, to better implement this decision by the Taliban group, the girls, especially the Afghan National Army widows, will be married to the Taliban fighters.

# Unknown Man

With the Taliban's arrival in Kabul on August 2021, many families forced their daughters under 18 to marry for fear of being raped by Taliban fighters. Some families sold their daughters due to economic poverty, creating a hot market for sex abusers. Despite these bitter and shocking events, all these anomalies and voids in Kabul heavily burdened and pressured Najiba's soul and spirit. One day, when Najiba checked her Facebook account, she noticed a message from an unknown man who claimed he was a businessman in Kuwait City and offered to help Najiba.

She received a long message from an unknown man on her Facebook messenger, which directly addressed her "Hello dear Najiba! I am a businessman living in the beautiful city of Kuwait. I have been following your Facebook account for a while now. To say you are a good and intelligent girl. However, I'm so sorry for the unexpected situation happened in Afghanistan." This anonymous man continued to write, "I have already helped several civil and women's rights activist girls to get out of Afghanistan. Now that the Taliban group is ruling in the cities, I felt it necessary to give you the offer to leave Kabul city, and I hope you will accept this humanitarian proposal."

"So, I want to say that as a human being and an Afghan man, I feel the pain and suffering of my fellow countrymen and women in my heart. I consider myself responsible for helping you and your family escape those bad conditions in Kabul and be transferred to a safe place." At the end of his message, he wrote to Najiba, "If you want to get more information, please send me a message on my telegram account so that we can talk more about the issue. I will be very pleased to be able to help you and your family."

After reading this message, Najiba put her phone away and continued with her daily activities, but this message bothered her mind. Najiba said to herself with great concern, "Maybe this anonymous message would be like a lottery option for at least once. He may be an honest man and wants to help us. Although he was not so young in terms of age, he is almost as old as my grandfather."

Najiba was a girl with high dreams and goals; because of her hard work and ambitions, like all other girls, she received many offers for friendship, marriage, and sometimes for sex when she was a student at the universities of Ghazni. But she didn't care about all these requests and made sharper the greed of many people who were looking for sex and abuse to use any option to satisfy her.

So, sometimes people looking for sex would mediate one of Najiba's classmates, and sometimes they would warn that they would defame her on social networks.

But she fought without paying attention to all these challenges, injustices, gender, and racial discrimination to study. A few days after that first message on Facebook, Najiba received another message from the unknown man who wrote, "I am waiting for you in this beautiful city, dear Najiba." But now, she was suspicious about how eager this unknown old man was to help me!

Therefore, Najiba hesitantly sent him a message via Telegram: "Hello, I am Najiba, you said to send me a message on Telegram, I want to know the details of your help and cooperation, and if you can explain it, I would be grateful."

This unknown man immediately replied, "Thank you very much, dear Najiba, for sending me a message. He told Najiba all his arranged and evil plans and that he would save her from the evil of Kabul city. Najiba, who had doubts, sometimes felt it like a lottery chance and sometimes blamed herself.

In all his words, the unknown man complimented Najiba on how intelligent and beautiful a girl she was and deserved the best life and peace in a city like Kuwait. In a conversation with Najiba, the unknown man said you have a bright future and will be a pity in this country with the Taliban's dominance. Little by little, the nasty inner words of an unknown man almost convinced Najiba in the name of humanitarian aid. Since Najiba was in such a situation, these words were pleasing and equally painful for her. The unknown man told Najiba that he would pay all her education expenses after moving to the beautiful city of Kuwait. Najiba witnessed all these unfortunate events when the Taliban came to the cities of Afghanistan. However, the promise of such a life was a wish for her. But the offer of this help cast a shadow of doubt and a great apprehension in her mind.

# "Najiba Asked Herself"

Why will all this cooperation be being offered to me for no reason?

Isn't it because I'm a young girl and still a virgin?

Or is this unknown man sincere that he wants to help me?

# 10 The Heart-Wrenching August

# Rescue Or Entrapment?

There weren't answers. All of Najiba's thoughts were filled with unanswered and annoying questions. Najiba was confused and worried about her and her family's safety in Kabul because her brother was a member of the Afghan National Army. In addition, they were a family from the Hazara community, and the Taliban has always sought to kill Hazaras in Afghanistan without any excuse. On the other hand, she listened to this man's words and messages with hesitation, thought about the opportunity, and wondered whether this was an option to save or trap?

On the one hand, Najiba was hesitant by all these charming words from the unknown man. On the other hand, she had great fears that the Taliban might come and kill her family because her brother was a member of the National Army. Therefore, Najiba believed the words of an unidentified man in this situation, even though she was worried from all sides. This unknown man determined the meeting place with her during a phone call. Based on this, Najiba should hand over all her and her family's identification documents in one place for a visa to leave Kabul.

# Kārte Parwān Place Of Trapping

A few minutes later, her phone rang, and she reluctantly picked up the phone and heard the thick voice of a man saying: "Hello, dear Najiba!". Najiba, whose heart was trembling, composed herself and talked to him. The unknown man told her that "Najiba! Tomorrow, bring all the documents of yourself and your family to the Kārte Parwān, so that I can process the visa for you to leave Kabul." Kārte Parwān is a neighborhood in the north-western of Kabul city. She listened to this man's words hoping to get help and escape the fear and terror of Kabul by the Taliban group. She agreed to take all her documents to the desired address in Kārte Parwān tomorrow, hoping luck would help her.

That night, Najiba made the final decision and said that might luck would be with her and she could get rid of the suffocating situation of Kabul city under the Taliban rule. So, the next day, Najiba went to the address the unknown man had told her. When she got to Kārte Parwān, she called the strange man and said, "I brought all the documents. Where are you?" The unidentified man, in the role of a businessman, replied to her, "Wait there a few minutes, until I come and get the documents from you."

After a few moments passed, Najiba was surrounded by Taliban fighters. The Taliban fighters came to her with red eyes, long hair, and horrible looks. She was stunned with fear, and her whole body was shaking with fear. Luck was no longer with Najiba anymore. And everything turned into blackness and darkness moments for her.

He was a cunning man, neither a businessman nor a humanitarian aid worker. The photo in his Facebook account was not his own, but a fake photo. The unknown man was one of the Taliban commanders who had been looking for Najiba's family for a long time because her brother was a member of the Afghan National Army. Najiba's story is nothing new, and the Taliban has always had virtual space groups that trap military personnel and their opponents in various ways.

# The Heart-Wrenching August

In August 2021, Najiba was trapped by the cyberspace jihadists of the Taliban group and kidnapped from Karte Parwan in Kabul city, Afghanistan. The Taliban took her to prison because her brother was a national army soldier in the previous Afghan government. The Taliban has committed many atrocities against Najiba to surrender her brother to the Taliban regime. But she didn't know about her brother anymore as he'd been hiding in fear of the Taliban group ever since the Taliban came to Kabul and the previous government collapsed. This was the saddest and heart-wrenching August that the people of Afghanistan, especially women and girls, have ever experienced.

According to the extreme jihadists of the Taliban group, the crime of Najiba's family was heavy and severe. For a reason, her brother was a member of the national army; on the other hand, this family was from the religious and ethnic minorities of the Hazara community, which the Taliban have persecuted, tortured, and killed Hazaras in Afghanistan throughout history.

Another horrible tragedy and inhumane violence by Taliban jihadist fighters broke the hearts of millions of people throughout Kabul city and Afghanistan. This brutal tragedy is the story of an atrocious crime against Najiba and her dear brother. She was a young girl who was tricked by extremists of the Taliban group on Facebook and kidnapped from Karte Parwan. After a few days, her dead body was handed over to her family. She had been brutally tortured, harassed, and even repeatedly raped. This sadness is not so tiny; the sadness that plunged a community, a family, and a generation into sad silence.

# Brutal And Inhuman Tortures

The Taliban interrogated Najiba in jail because her brother was a member of the Afghan National Army. She had to show the address and location of her brother to the Taliban intelligence department. But since the Taliban came to cities, her brother had fled home and hid in fear. Even Najiba did not know where her brother was. Hence the jihadi criminals of the Taliban spared nothing against that young girl and subjected her to mental and emotional torture, beating, and even sexual assault until they killed her in prison for being a Hazara. Najiba's story did not end with her death in the Taliban jail cells, but her sad story saddened her family and all the neighbors and people of Kabul city.

Najiba's whole body was brutally tortured in the Taliban jail cells. All the signs of bruises, torture, rape and her fingernails were pulled out. It was evident that even one of her breasts was cut off by the Taliban during interrogation and torture in the jail. Najiba's story ends with her death, but the unfortunate and bitter consequences of this story make the people of Kabul city suffer every day and night, and her family is also mourning her young daughter.

Due to the arrival of the Taliban group in 2021, Afghan women and girls commit self-immolation and suicide every day to be freed from oppression and atrocities under Taliban rule. Therefore, killings and crimes against women and army soldiers by the Taliban and their operatives are rampant in all regions of Afghanistan, especially in Kabul city.

Despite such a brutal and inhumane crime against Najiba, the Taliban were not satisfied, eventually leading to her death. The main target of the Taliban group was her army brother, who always hunted him down to kill him. These crimes can be caused by hate and terrorist thoughts occurring in this territory. And finally, after some time, bloodthirsty hunters killed Najiba's brother, who was a member of the National Army, on November 2023, in the west of Kabul city. Then they took his body hostage. —hoping for a day when no women, girls, and young soldiers in this city will not be victims of war crimes and terrorism.

**(Non-fiction)**

## About the Author

**Asadullah Jafari "Pezhman"**

Asadullah Jafari "Pezhman" is a Translator, Columnist, and a former member of the Afghan National Army, born in 1998, from Afghanistan. He often writes and translates on Afghanistan and the Middle East issues. Asadullah has also worked as a translator and columnist for SubheKabul Newspaper, Jade-Abresham Weekly, Indian Defence Review, Tribune Zamaneh, and Hindu Post. His most famous works of translation are the book "Tears from Kabul and Deliverance from Kabul" translated from English into Persian/Dari. Hence, Asadullah was Honored and Deserved Appreciation in Special Section for the 3rd Iranian Youth Book of the Year National Award as an Immigrant Young in 2023.

**Mrs. Pamela Hart**, based in New York City, is a Poet, Editor, Teacher, and Author of the award-winning poetry collection Mothers Over Nangarhar, and she has also contributed to the editing of this work.

www.ingramcontent.com/pod-product-compliance
Lightning Source LLC
LaVergne TN
LVHW041603070526
838199LV00047B/2112